NINJA VS. SKELETONS

**WRITTEN BY
CLAIRE SIPI**

BONE RATTLING BATTLES

THE PILOT SEASON of NINJAGO™: Masters of Spinjitzu sees the rise of Lord Garmadon. Master Wu trains four ninja to help him defeat his evil brother. However, Garmadon is not alone—he has a mighty Skeleton Army. A total of 16 awesome LEGO® sets bring this season's characters, weapons, vehicles, and locations to life. Turn the page to find out more...

To find out more about this minifigure see p.20.

HOW TO USE THIS BOOK

This book is a guide to the LEGO® NINJAGO™ minifigures from the pilot season. Learn all about the ninja and their different personalities, plus the scary foes they must battle.

CONTENTS

MASTER WU

SPINJITZU MASTER

NINJA FILE

LIKES: Drinking tea
DISLIKES: Evil siblings throwing tantrums
FRIENDS: New recruits
FOES: Lord Garmadon
SKILLS: Wisdom
GEAR: Bo staff

SET NAME: Master Wu, Fire Temple, Lightning Dragon Battle
SET NUMBER: 2255, 2507, 2521
YEAR: 2011

Master Wu's beard and mustache are removable.

Magical golden writing protects Master Wu from evil.

BROTHERLY BOTHER

Master Wu and his brother, Lord Garmadon, were trained by their father, the First Spinjitzu Master. He hoped that his sons would use their skills to protect the people of Ninjago Island. Lord Garmadon uses his powers for evil, but Wu carries on his father's noble legacy.

MASTER OF THE POWER of creation, Wu is the son of the First Spinjitzu Master who created Ninjago Island. As well as mastering the ancient martial art of Spinjitzu, wise Master Wu has achieved the ultimate power. He can control all four elements—fire, ice, lightning, and earth.

COLE
MASTER OF EARTH

NINJA FILE

LIKES: Extreme sports
DISLIKES: Dancing
FRIENDS: Fellow ninja
FOES: Kruncha, Chopov
SKILLS: Strength
GEAR: Bow and arrow, hammer

SET NAME: Cole, Turbo Shredder, Ninja Training Outpost
SET NUMBER: 2112, 2263, 2516
YEAR: 2011

Golden emblem showing the Earth symbol

Bow and arrow for target practice

TEAM FIRST
Cole was the first student Master Wu recruited for ninja training. Cole enjoys focusing his energy and powers during Wu's grueling training routines. Target practice helps him improve his concentration and accuracy.

COLE IS AS STRONG and reliable as a rock. His natural strategic and leadership skills make him a key part of the ninja team. Cole always puts his team first and is a true friend to the other ninja. Cole can spin dirt and soil into a huge storm, reducing everything in its path to dust.

KAI
MASTER OF FIRE

Traditional head wrap made from two scarves to leave only the eyes uncovered

DID YOU KNOW?

Kai's father may have known the secrets of the ninja. He guarded a map that showed the location of four powerful weapons.

Katana sword was forged in Kai's blacksmith shop.

Sashes and belts are an essential part of a ninja's outfit.

FAMILY HISTORY

Kai and his sister, Nya, took over the Four Weapons Blacksmith Shop when their father died. Wu saw that Kai had the potential to be more than a blacksmith and trained him to use his natural "fire" to master Spinjitzu.

THIS NINJA'S ELEMENT is fire and his temper is equally hot! Kai accepts Master Wu's challenge to train as a ninja, but he must work hard to control his anger and impatience. Master Wu's faith in Kai is justified—he soon becomes a brave, loyal, and skillful ninja. He channels his fiery energy into Spinjitzu.

JAY
MASTER OF LIGHTNING

NINJA FILE

LIKES: Witty jokes
DISLIKES: Broken technology
FRIENDS: Nya
FOES: Nuckal, Krazi
SKILLS: Inventing
GEAR: Spear, katana

SET NAME: Jay, Skull Motorbike, Turbo Shredder, Skull Truck, Ninja Training, Jay
SET NUMBER: 2257, 2259, 2263, 2506, 30082, 30084
YEAR: 2011

Nunchucks of Lightning are one of the four Golden Weapons.

Golden emblem on robe is the symbol for lightning.

LIGHTNING SPINJITZU
Jay was the first of the four ninja to master the art of Spinjitzu. Now, as quick as a flash, he can spin to turn into a lightning tornado crackling with electric ninja energy.

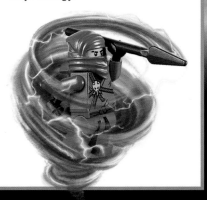

LIGHTNING IS HIS ELEMENT and Jay is lightning-fast in combat. His flair for crazy inventions, his thirst for adventure, and his sense of humor are just some of the qualities that Master Wu knew would make Jay a good, skillful ninja. Jay is also creative and loves solving problems.

Zane's ninja wrap is as icy white as his element.

NINJA FILE

LIKES: Cooking
DISLIKES: Jokes
FRIENDS: Master Wu
FOES: Wyplash, Bonezai
SKILLS: Logic
GEAR: Katana sword, flat spear

SET NAME: Zane, Spinjitzu Dojo, Skull Truck, Fire Temple, Ninja Glider
SET NUMBER: 2113, 2504, 2506, 2507, 30080
YEAR: 2011

NINJA GLIDER

In Ninja Glider (set 30080), Zane has a super cool Ninja Glider made from six golden blades. Zane can silently glide up on his enemies armed with a lethal black katana.

Black hands contrast with Zane's white robes, but are featured on all the ninja recruits.

ZANE IS QUIET, serious, and focused. He learns quickly and is curious about everything. Zane watches and waits for the right moment to strike. He is so quiet and stealthy that he can creep up on his enemies without being detected. However, his friends' jokes often pass him by undetected in return!

NYA

SISTER OF KAI

Nya can use many different weapons, including daggers.

NINJA FILE

LIKES: Her independence
DISLIKES: Being kidnapped
FRIENDS: Jay
FOES: Skeleton Army
SKILLS: Tech wiz
GEAR: Daggers, staff

SET NAME: Nya, Garmadon's Dark Fortress, Fire Temple
SET NUMBER: 2172, 2505, 2507
YEAR: 2011

SECRETIVE SISTER

Nya hides her identity so that she can help the ninja, but is she also keeping secrets from them? When the Skeleton Army kidnap Nya, she soon shows the sneaky Skulkins that she has warrior skills of her own.

Red veil covers Nya's determined expression.

Robes with phoenix detail are printed on legs

DID YOU KNOW?

Nya was the first LEGO NINJAGO minifigure to have a double-sided head. She was followed by Lloyd, P.I.X.A.L., and many others.

NYA IS KAI'S younger sister. She works with Kai in the Four Weapons Blacksmith Shop. Although she isn't a ninja yet, tough Nya is determined to be better than the boys. She trains hard and, with a veil to mask her identity, she is always ready to battle evil. She uses her skills with computers to spy on their enemies.

LORD GARMADON

MASTER OF DESTRUCTION

Underworld helmet helps to control the Skeleton Army.

Thunder Bolt weapon can zap foes with electricity.

NINJA FILE

LIKES: Evil plans
DISLIKES: Meddling ninja
FRIENDS: None
FOES: Great Devourer
SKILLS: Arguing with Wu
GEAR: Thunder Bolt, Underworld helmet

SET NAME: Lord Garmadon, Garmadon's Dark Fortress, Skull Truck, Fire Temple
SET NUMBER: 2256, 2505, 2506, 2507
YEAR: 2011

THE GREAT DEVOURER

Garmadon wasn't always bad. He was bitten by a snake called the Great Devourer as a child, and its venom made him evil. After losing a duel with Wu, Garmadon developed his evil appearance and fell into the Underworld.

MASTER WU'S EVIL brother, Lord Garmadon, is King of the Underworld. With the help of his Skeleton Army, he continues to spread fear on his dark quest to defeat his brother and the ninja, and to destroy Ninjago Island. He has trained the boneheaded Skeletons in the ways of Spinjitzu, making them fearsome opponents.

MASTER WU
DOJO LEADER

DID YOU KNOW?

This version of Master Wu wears a black belt. In most martial arts, a black belt means that the wearer has reached expert level.

Traditional conical hat shades Wu's eyes from the sun.

Head is printed with wise eyes and gray eyebrows.

NINJA FILE

LIKES: Riddles
DISLIKES: Sleeping ninja
FRIENDS: Ninja students
FOES: Skeleton Army
SKILLS: Endless patience
GEAR: Bo staff

SET NAME: Spinjitzu Dojo, Ninjago Battle Arena, Exclusive Weapon Training Set
SET NUMBER: 2504, 853106, 853111
YEAR: 2011

Clean white robes are Wu's training uniform.

TIME FOR TEA?
Teaching four young ninja-in-training can be thirsty work! Master Wu schedules regular breaks for a refreshing cup of tea. These are often just for Wu though—the ninja must keep busy!

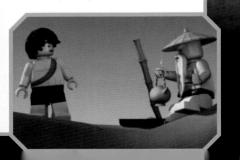

MASTER WU MAY BE very old, but he is an expert ninja and a fearless warrior. He plans to pass on his valuable knowledge to a new generation of ninja. Master Wu makes his students train every day, and tells them to use their brains as well as their strength. Without wisdom you can't win.

SAMUKAI

GENERAL OF FIRE

Wide, open mouth is unique in LEGO NINJAGO minifigures.

Unique skull markings

NINJA FILE

LIKES: Being in charge
DISLIKES: Following orders
FRIENDS: Fellow generals
FOES: Lord Garmadon
SKILLS: Plotting schemes
GEAR: Bone daggers

SET NAME: Garmadon's Dark Fortress, Fire Temple
SET NUMBER: 2505, 2507
YEAR: 2011

MEETING THEIR MATCH

The four trainee ninja each represent a different element, and so do their bony foes. Samukai is linked with Fire, just like Kai. Sparks fly when the pair battle, thanks to their blazing blades!

One of four bony arms allow him to wield four weapons at once

ONCE THE KING of the Underworld, Samukai's reign was overthrown by Lord Garmadon. Now, the fearsome Samukai leads the Skeleton Army in its battle against the ninja, under Garmadon's control. Garmadon plans to use four-armed Samukai to wield the four Golden Weapons.

KRUNCHA

GENERAL OF EARTH

Sophisticated Kruncha wears a monocle on his right eye.

Standard skeleton torso fits under removable armor.

Jagged golden blade is heavy and sharp.

BODY ARMOR

Kruncha's protective body armor is different to that of most other Skulkins. The shoulder pads are heavier and he doesn't wear the gray chest panel with markings on it. Only Wyplash has armor similar to Kruncha's.

LOUD, HARD, AND STRONG, Kruncha is one of the four generals in the Skeleton Army. The General of Earth, Kruncha is mean and will crush anyone who dares to get in his way. He often shouts at his foot soldiers, but is also constantly bickering with fellow general, Nuckal.

WYPLASH

GENERAL OF ICE

NINJA FILE

LIKES: Keeping watch
DISLIKES: Not knowing what is going on
FRIENDS: He trusts no one
FOES: Watchful Nya
SKILLS: Stealth
GEAR: Stolen scythe blade

SET NAME: Wyplash, Skull Truck, Earth Dragon Defence
SET NUMBER: 2175, 2506, 2509
YEAR: 2011

Shoulder pad and body protection armor

Sword with sharp curved blade

Black feet on LEGO NINJAGO skeletons differ from those on traditional LEGO skeletons.

SKULL DECORATION

Wyplash wears a bamboo hat, just like Master Wu's! Wyplash is the only Skeleton General with removable headwear. He is also the only Skeleton who has a worm crawling from the side of his skull!

Worm could be the cause of Wyplash's headaches.

WYPLASH IS A GENERAL in Garmadon's Army and Samukai's second-in-command. Stealth is his special skill, and he always watches and waits for the right moment to attack his enemy. Paranoid Wyplash can turn his huge skull backwards, which means he can always see the enemy approaching.

NUCKAL
GENERAL OF LIGHTNING

DID YOU KNOW?

The four Skeleton Generals are the only Skeleton minifigures to have proper skull-shaped head pieces.

Nuckal's skull is a unique molded piece with a row of head spikes.

Metal eye patch

NINJA FILE

LIKES: Causing mayhem

DISLIKES: Being bored

FRIENDS: Skeletons of Lightning

FOES: Anyone in his way

SKILLS: Bravery

GEAR: Silver dark blade

SET NAME: Nuckal, Nuckal's ATV, Spinjitzu Dojo

SET NUMBER: 2173, 2518, 2504

YEAR: 2011

ALL-TERRAIN TERROR

Nuckal's ATV (All-Terrain Vehicle) causes destruction wherever it goes. This scary bone buggy packs a punch with its heavy armor, solid suspension, and missile launcher. It is to be avoided at all costs!

NUCKAL IS CHILDISH, wild, and very dangerous. He loves fighting, and if there is trouble to be found, Nuckal will find it! This bony brute's idea of fun is striking ninja down with his lightning-fast battle skills. His lethal moves are often combined with a cackling and electrifying laugh.

FRAKJAW

SKELETON OF FIRE

DID YOU KNOW?
Despite owning a sturdy helmet, Frakjaw drives the Turbo Shredder (set 2263) wearing only a bamboo hat for protection!

NINJA FILE

LIKES: Chatting
DISLIKES: Being bored
FRIENDS: Krazi—he is the only Skeleton brave enough!
FOES: Fire Ninja Kai
SKILLS: Fearless nature
GEAR: Golden mace, dark blade, long bone

SET NAME: Skeleton Chopper, Spinjitzu Starter Set, Lightning Dragon Battle, Turbo Shredder
SET NUMBER: 30081, 2257, 2521, 2263
YEAR: 2011

Helmet with goggles protects Frakjaw in battle.

WEAPONS STASH

The Skeletons have a terrifying collection of weapons to use in battle. The ninja need all their skills to defeat this evil enemy. They are brutal and vicious fighters, and the legendary Frakjaw is one of the worst of all.

Golden mace increases Frakjaw's attack range when he launches into his Spinjitzu moves.

THIS SCARY RED-ROBED Skeleton is the toughest Skulkin in Lord Garmadon's army. He is fiery and angry and loves to fight—especially with the ninja! Frakjaw loves the sound of his own voice and sometimes it is difficult to get him to shut up. He especially likes to taunt and challenge his enemies.

KRAZI
SKELETON OF LIGHTNING

NINJA FILE

LIKES: Making trouble
DISLIKES: Being serious
FRIENDS: Frakjaw
FOES: Lightning Ninja Jay
SKILLS: Speedy reactions
GEAR: Bone, pickax

SET NAME: Krazi, Ice Dragon Attack
SET NUMBER: 2116, 2260
YEAR: 2011

DID YOU KNOW?

It isn't only ninja that are mastering the art of Spinjitzu. Krazi's Lightning tornado is terrifying and fast!

Removable jester's hat in red and blue

Red face paint completes the clownish look.

Stolen Shuriken of Ice

POINTED PROTECTION

Krazi minifigures feature either a red and blue jester's hat or blue armor, never both. Krazi's blue shoulder spikes match those on the armor of his Lightning General, Nuckal.

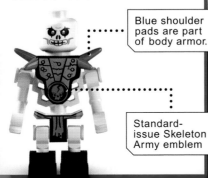

Blue shoulder pads are part of body armor.

Standard-issue Skeleton Army emblem

KRAZI BY NAME and crazy by nature, this wild menace is a Skulkin warrior in Lord Garmadon's Skeleton Army. Krazi is the fastest of the Skeletons—when he strikes he is lightning quick. Krazi's red and blue jester's hat and red face paint are signs of his crazy personality.

CHOPOV
SKELETON OF EARTH

DID YOU KNOW?

There are multiple versions of the Chopov minifigure. Other variants have a gray sash and gray shoulder spikes.

Black military helmet

Bone ax

Other Chopov variants have loincloth printing on the hips.

NINJA FILE

LIKES: Dreaming big
DISLIKES: Flat tires
FRIENDS: Skeletons of Earth
FOES: Earth Ninja Cole
SKILLS: Engineering
GEAR: Bronzed bone ax

SET NAME: Chopov, Skull Motorbike, Garmadon's Dark Fortress
SET NUMBER: 2114, 2259, 2505
YEAR: 2011

SKULL MOTORBIKE

Chopov's battle vehicle from set 2259 is a cool chopper motorbike. He uses it in battle or for quick escapes. The powerful skull hammerhead can smash anything in its path, especially ninja!

Catapult hinge mechanism

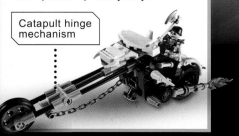

CHOPOV IS AS TOUGH as a rock. Chopov doesn't let anything get in his way, even ninja! This smart warrior is also the chief mechanic of the Skeleton Army and maintains all of the vehicles. He secretly wishes that he, instead of Bonezai, could design the Skeleton Army's super cool vehicles.

BONEZAI

SKELETON OF ICE

NINJA FILE

LIKES: Villainous vehicles

DISLIKES: Bad drivers

FRIENDS: Chopov—or so he thinks!

FOES: Ice Ninja Zane

SKILLS: Inventing

GEAR: Silver bone ax

SET NAME: Bonezai, Ninja Ambush, Garmadon's Dark Fortress, Ninjago Battle Arena

SET NUMBER: 2115, 2258, 2505, 2520

YEAR: 2011

Don't let his smile fool you—Bonezai is a true threat!

Battle-scarred torso printing

Snowy white sash represents Bonezai's icy nature.

SNEAK ATTACK

Bonezai's head is printed with crossed eyes—perhaps as a result of a surprise blow to the head from Kai. Can Bonezai keep his cool, or will he not be able to stand the heat of Kai's attack?

BONEZAI DESIGNS all of the vehicles that the Skeleton Army use in battle. This stealthy warrior is as cold as ice and strikes a chill into the hearts of his enemies. He is so cold he can even freeze shadows! Bonezai uses his ice element abilities to win weapons and battle for glory.

KAI DX

FIRE DRAGON EXTREME

Kai's hood is unchanged from his training uniform.

Golden Fire Dragon printed on robe breathes the element of fire.

NINJA FILE

LIKES: Flying fast on Flame

DISLIKES: Losing dragon races

FRIENDS: Flame

FOES: Skeleton Army

SKILLS: Dragon-whispering

GEAR: Sword of Fire

SET NAME: Fire Temple, Mountain Shrine, Nuckal's ATV

SET NUMBER: 2507, 2254, 2518

YEAR: 2011

Kai uses a normal sword before mastering his Golden Weapon.

MASTER OF FIRE

Kai received his new ninja dragon robe after he had found his dragon and mastered the Sword of Fire. This was one of the four Golden Weapons that belonged to the First Spinjitzu Master.

KAI HAS MANAGED to tame his dragon and has gained DX (Dragon eXtreme) ranking and a new ninja dragon costume to match. Kai first enlisted the help of his dragon when the ninja needed to travel to the Underworld. Kai was able to encourage his dragon to use its incredible speed to fly to Master Wu's aid.

FIRE DRAGON
FIRE GUARDIAN

DID YOU KNOW?
At a certain point in their lives, the ninja's dragons must fly away and shed their scales (molt) in order to become adult dragons.

Flaming tip of tail can be used to attack enemies.

Jaws of fiery head contain a red-hot weapons launcher

THIS MIGHTY FIRE DRAGON guards the Golden Sword of Fire, which Master Wu hid in the Fire Temple. When Kai tames this dragon, he is able to control and ride him. Kai names his dragon Flame—a fitting name for a creature who is red-hot from nose to tail!

HIDDEN DRAGON
The Fire Temple set conceals the mighty Fire Dragon. Flame's wings are just visible when the temple is closed, but when open, Flame appears in all his blazing glory.

JAY DX
LIGHTNING DRAGON EXTREME

Distinctive
eyebrows give
Jay's identity
away.

New dark blue
obi sash

DRAGON CHAMPION
When the ninja aren't out fighting
Skeletons, they make sure their
dragons still get plenty of
exercise. The ninja have regular
races around the Ninjago skies.
Jay loves to win—and celebrate!

JAY USED HIS INVENTING SKILLS to tame
his dragon when his jokes and cooking failed
to win the dragon over. He created a dragon
roar amplifier to boost the volume of his
dragon's battle cry. Now, with his DX ninja
status and the Nunchucks of Lightning, Jay
is more than ready to do battle against evil.

LIGHTNING DRAGON
LIGHTNING GUARDIAN

Two long spears mounted on the dragon's wings

Deadly flicking tail delivers a nasty shock to foes.

NINJA FILE

LIKES: Thunderstorms
DISLIKES: Solid ground
FRIENDS: Jay
FOES: Pigeons
SKILLS: Electric shocks
GEAR: Wing-mounted spears

SET NAME: Lightning Dragon Battle
SET NUMBER: 2521
YEAR: 2011

Claw with golden talons is attached to the dragon's wing.

FLYING FLAGS
The two flags Wisp carries feature the Japanese symbols for "dragon god." In Japan, dragons are known as "tatsu," or "ryu," and blue dragons symbolize the East of the country.

龍
神

THIS LIGHTNING DRAGON guards the Golden Nunchucks of Lightning, which Master Wu hid in the desolate Floating Ruins. Jay names his dragon Wisp and once tamed, Wisp is forever loyal to Jay. Wisp shares Jay's electric powers and lightning-fast reactions.

COLE DX
EARTH DRAGON EXTREME

DID YOU KNOW?

Cole's DX ninja robes have his name and earth elemental symbol on the back. The other ninja have similar back patterns.

Scythe of Quakes is linked to the earth element.

Earth Dragon's huge scaly tail is printed on the legs.

MOVING MOTIVATION

The quickest way to Cole's heart is through his stomach, and it is the same for his dragon. Cole encourages the dragon to greater speeds by dangling a tasty roast chicken in front of his nose!

COLE HAS TO OVERCOME his biggest fear—dragons—to achieve his DX ninja status. With the courage of a true leader, Cole faces his fear and learns how to control his dragon. Against the odds, Cole becomes very fond of the beast. Next, Cole turns his attention to mastering the mighty Scythe of Quakes.

EARTH DRAGON

EARTH GUARDIAN

NINJA FILE

LIKES: Crushing villains
DISLIKES: Fancy flying manuevers
FRIENDS: Cole
FOES: Puny skeletons
SKILLS: Destruction
GEAR: Boulder-swinging tail

SET NAME: Earth Dragon Defence
SET NUMBER: 2509
YEAR: 2011

Flags attach to the harness Cole uses to ride Rocky.

DID YOU KNOW?
Rocky is the only Elemental Dragon with four legs and two small wings. The others have two legs and larger, clawed wings.

龍神

龍神

Powerful jaw fires stone missiles at enemies.

ARMORED BEAST
Rocky's legs and wings are protected with armored scales and he has spikes on his body. His horned head is made from a different mold to the other dragons, to match his bulky body.

THIS AWESOME Earth Dragon guards the Scythe of Quakes, which Master Wu hid in the Caves of Despair. He is the first of the Elemental Dragons that the ninja encounter in their search for the Golden Weapons. When Cole learns to control the Earth Dragon, he names him Rocky.

ZANE DX
ICE DRAGON EXTREME

Removable hood disguises Zane's face.

Ice Dragon breathes out freezing blasts of ice.

NINJA FILE

LIKES: Following directions
DISLIKES: Getting lost
FRIENDS: Shard
FOES: Frakjaw and friends
SKILLS: Spinjitzu skills
GEAR: Black katana sword, Shurikens of Ice

SET NAME: Zane DX, Ice Dragon Attack
SET NUMBER: 2171, 2260
YEAR: 2011

TAKE THE REINS

Zane has such exceptional balance that he can perch on the back of his dragon without a saddle! Zane clears some ice from the creature's back and guides him with two metal reins.

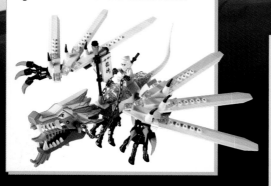

ZANE'S FIRST MEETING with his dragon didn't go very well—the beast froze Zane into a solid block of ice! As soon as he had thawed out, Zane was able to tame the dragon and earn his DX (Dragon eXtreme) ninja status. Seeing this cool couple together sends chills down the spines of their Skeleton foes.

ICE DRAGON
ICE GUARDIAN

NINJA FILE

LIKES: Cool breezes
DISLIKES: Summer
FRIENDS: Zane
FOES: Fiery Skeleton vehicles
SKILLS: Freezing enemies
GEAR: Razor-sharp claws

SET NAME: Ice Dragon Attack
SET NUMBER: 2260
YEAR: 2011

Movable ice-feathered wings can be splayed out.

Raised spikes poke out of ice-coated wings.

DID YOU KNOW?
The Ice Dragon is the smallest of the four Elemental Dragons, but he is just as terrifying as his fellow beasts.

Ice ball is ready to fire.

FRESH BREATH
Icy breath shoots out from Shard's jaws, freezing everything in its path. Solid frozen ice balls can be fired at speed from this icy beast's terrifying jaws.

THIS ICE DRAGON guards the Golden Shurikens of Ice, which Master Wu hid inside the Ice Fortress in the Frozen Wasteland. After a frosty first encounter, Zane uses his elemental powers to find a connection with the mythical beast. He tames the dragon and names him Shard.

Penguin
Random
House

Project Editor Emma Grange
Senior Designers Jo Connor, Mark Penfound
Editors Arushi Vats, Rosie Peet, Matt Jones,
Clare Millar
Designers Radhika Banerjee, Dimple Vohra,
Stefan Georgiou
Editorial Assistants Beth Davies
Pre-Production Producer Kavita Varma
Senior Producer Lloyd Robertson
Editorial Managers Paula Regan,
Chitra Subramanyam
Design Managers Guy Harvey, Neha Ahuja
Creative Manager Sarah Harland
Art Director Lisa Lanzarini
Publisher Julie Ferris
Publishing Director Simon Beecroft

First American Edition, 2016
Published in the United States by DK Publishing
345 Hudson Street, New York, New York 10014
DK, a Division of Penguin Random House LLC

Contains content previously published in LEGO®
NINJAGO™ *Character Encyclopedia Updated and Expanded
Edition* (2016)

001–298874–Jul/16

ACKNOWLEDGEMENTS
DK would like to thank Randi Sørensen, Martin Leighton Lindhart,
Paul Hansford, Madeline Boushie, Simon Lucas, Nicolaas Johan Bernardo
Vás, and Daniel McKenna at the LEGO Group, Gary Ombler for extra
photography, Andy Jones for extra editorial help, Sam Bartlett for
design assistance and Claire Sipi for her writing. For the original edition
of this book, DK would like to thank Shari Last, Julia March, Ruth Amos,
Lauren Rosier, Mark Richards, Jon Hall, Clive Savage,
Ron Stobbart, and Catherine Saunders.

www.LEGO.com

www.dk.com
A WORLD OF IDEAS:
SEE ALL THERE IS TO KNOW